Call The Catastrophists

Call The Catastrophists

Krystal Languell

BlazeVOX [books]
Buffalo, NY

CALL THE CATASTROPHISTS
by Krystal Languell   Copyright © 2011
Published by BlazeVOX [books]

Printed in the United States of America
Book design by Geoffrey Gatza
First Edition
ISBN: 978-1-60964-090-3
Library of Congress Control Number: 2011911560

BlazeVOX [books]
76 Inwood Place
Buffalo, NY 14209

Editor@blazevox.org

publisher of weird little books

BlazeVOX [books]

blazevox.org

2   4   6   8   0   9   7   5   3   1

BlazeVOX

Acknowledgments

Some of these poems appeared previously in the following journals:

H_NGM_N, Santa Clara Review, Caesura, sous rature, No Tell Motel, DIAGRAM, Splinter Generation, La Petite Zine, Delirious Hem, Everyday Genius, Lingerpost, Fairy Tale Review and in the chapbooks *The Mean Particle* (Tilt Press) and *many lost cause creatures* (Dusie).

For my sister, Katrina
    I wish you high kicks and high fives.

TABLE OF CONTENTS

Call The Catastrophists

Many Lost Cause Creatures Could Form a Very Sad List

1.
Speak to the tender on bibliomancy.   His answer
is cunt in the surf—   cunt in the surf—   cunt in the surf.
We agree about death: "fuck that."   O Cigarettes, I may
be sick already so let's go on. In this case, time harms
          quickly since gin is a time machine.

2.
Afraid of bad news from the doctor but little else, coin
Dictator Witch   Find cat whiskers in the carpet—
          for my next cauldron of gendered magic,
let's go someplace necromantic.   Brad and I both drink
store brand Ensure because we don't want to *wither away*.

3.
Advanced degrees are not inherently evil but people
are working hard for change.   Every academic is guilty
of "my diamond shoes are too tight" logical fallacies. Should have
known—   should have known when Tyler warned me.

4.
His non-anatomical heart? Oh I don't give a shit. He wants
to get through it unscathed, this Friend of Poetry. Ten plus what?
You don't like pain, but a straight white man can't get
a dollar out of me—   The trouble with your defense
is I'm working class, too. Get in line and take a number.

5.
A conniption fit— this isn't Russia; it's a free country
with cheap food, too much meat. A deep freeze in every garage.
Will I know what killed me? The fish sticks   The hot dogs
cut up into mac and cheese   The burgers that crunched or the
Pillsbury Funfetti cupcakes— Halloween sprinkles out of season?

6.
You cultivate an image of your life like a Bikini Kill song
     like a Lunachick on diet pills, but what's the word for
an unemployed woman who lives with a man: *Domestic Goddess,
Engineer?* Ambien is your drug of choice & you lament like a Victorian.
Risk of chloroform poisoning not the only hamper to your productivity.

7.
Did Tyler mean   I'd think I could solve the problem?
     The problem now: Set it aside.
My rivalry with the future. A short memory, a sliding
sinker are the best weapons a starting pitcher can have.

8.
No subway scene microcosm, no list poem, no *from the mouths
of babes* moment— understand our worst little typographer,
     she was up all night listing insults, tearing collars.
Conversation's purpose: all charisma. Lacking that, it's too late
for the stiffest drink   To redeem an unfeeling body.

9.
We protect ourselves best together. You know sometimes
he gets the narrative wrong.   Drinking tea &
the so-called mortality problem.   Never responded, did he?
If he insists narrative, we know our role. *Like this, provider.*

10.
Do you have brain damage too? Me three. The short memory.
I miss Toledo.   I don't think Vespa scooters are sexy.
Do you mind hearing it again?   I just don't.
During commercials, forget what I'm watching. *Jersey Shore:*
I feel superior. *Golden Girls:* I feel empowered, rapt & unmoving.

11.
A slow talker says, "Where are the bodegas? In Brooklyn
you can go to a bodega   and get a Snapple." Indisputable.
& at the flea market you can buy milkman receipts & personal
              correspondence from 1907. The din in my museum
overpowers what's outside the window—it's old noise.

12.
Trend: scrolling through ringtones   Trend: bees trapped in the bus
Trend: high school fight songs   Trend: stoned at the Little Debbie display
Trend: dorm room porno   Trend: filesharing software / ethernet
Trend: shower stall sex   Trend: sometimes recycling batteries
Trend: the keg party tantrum   Trend: spring allergies blooming

13.
We met our first boyfriends in chat rooms when everyone
wanted to talk to strangers.   If our mothers knew
they'd've disconnected the AOL. Simon in New Orleans told me
about haunted houses, and yours sent you birthday mix tapes
with Bad Religion B-sides. Our least dangerous relationships.

14.
when you call on the poor to make donations
when you feel like a shelter dog
when I hear the word *culture* I reach for my checkbook
when I get my period on the way
to ship a dead woman's things home

CATASTROPHES

I Find A Way to Call Them Mine

When you call the catastrophists, be sure to remind them they're borrowing my vibration theory. In the moment just before disaster, movement sneaks up—not a siren but the absence of a siren—and then my famous pigtails wag the same way a paprika shaker breathes. Scientists ignore this kind of empirical evidence in their own lives, but they want my results. I want my facts back. I learned. Geologists would benefit from a lesson in gaze authenticity, the shameless plagiarists.

Post-Soviet

The problem of translation lives in morphologies. You must bear a table of equations, yet a spelling mistake changes those values. Then other words begin speaking— transliteration can be fun, but is usually wrong. You can only repeat your given letters. I showed Mother my slippery verb charts and she said *only your parents can truly be relied upon.* Mother is a soothsayer. *Don't ever be someone's workhorse,* she warns me.

Curatorial

The torture exhibit was gone the second time I went to the Danube Bend wax museum. King Mátyás was still at his table, the guests' eyeballs the sort that follow you as you walk by. No more, "pose in front of the thumbscrews; you're on vacation in Viségrad." Happy Austrians who paid to hear the narrative through headphones pushed the button that put it in German. Fewer of them now.

Homesickness I

I met an American man at the former Karl Marx University where one of two remaining
statues of Marx still stands and we would meet at Karl when we traveled in a large group
he bought a hat with communist buttons at the flea market we took a picture with a
bottle of wine in each hand—the hat on and cocked so he looked like our version of
native.

Homesickness II

On Wednesday night, after splitting a bottle of Alaszka vodka and crawling home, I dreamed about you. It's quick when I touch. You cooked with your shirt off and did my taxes while I drank whiskey and missed Indiana. You rearranged your furniture, approximating a distant relative's home. Please do something about the logic error of confession & I'll tell you the suffix for verbs from *I* to *you only* so that actions between us are one-word sentences.

Bratislava is the Capital of Slovakia

In the dog park, people called to their animals the same way I would later call you. Gyere ide *come here* was a pet call and you didn't like it. You phoned to invite me to Bratislava I didn't know what country that was in and stayed home. I tried to think of a complete sentence this summer but all I could come up with was és a többi, *and all the rest,* which is another way of telling you *blah blah blah.*

The alphabet is longer in some places extra letters, often vowels, are needed to put a finer point on emotional or romantic speech. For example, legyen szíves means *please.* Szives means nothing and I mean it is not a word, but szivacs means *sponge.* What is said literally for *please* is *do be with your heart:* the imperative form of "to be" with the adjectival form of "heart," whereas *I love you* is more concise.

Your Name Day

Kérek ital means *I want a drink.* Two boys wanted a tequila shot to share and we wanted to play conduit. May is the month when drink prices go up because the weather is nicer and we were all together: RJ, Csaba, and Jessica who took a cab across Hungary without any shoes. I got the money for Budapest from an insurance settlement, and at a simple conversion rate. Near the end I earned the title of Best Comeback then saw the Laci Peterson trial on television, wondered, "Who is this Laszló Peterson?"

If You Want It

We land behind schedule and to ask for directions, I lead him into a dance school where thirty adults are learning to waltz. He understands German but can't speak; Vienna is incidental, only a catastrophe if you want it. The beginning of my slow education in not having control: melodrama. My tears make the hotel concierge laugh and I spend five dollars to send an email filled with diacritical errors.

I release a pigeon in a small room and am attacked. A hunk of my upper arm torn out bone exposed I see that it's deep but put off tending the wound to give my sister a ride home. If dreams aren't literal I'm in trouble because the opposite is my not feeling martyr *enough* later realize it was my tattoo ripped out should not write publicly about dreams the internet is no place for the displaced subconscious.

I Told You About That

You don't need to remember the definition of *lie of omission* because you are surrounded by examples in language and action. The lover is gone again. Did I also forget to mention when you'll start your retail therapy? After her miscarriage my friend said *I need to look at things on racks then I'll start feeling better* department stores make me dizzy, swollen, nose starts to run but there is something more crucial I'm not telling yet.

Diaspora aside, I resign myself to illogical allegiance. *I kiss your hand* is nothing but a scrapbook page. My grandfather from Sopron near the border with Austria where they voted to stay Hungarian and became "the most loyal city." This much I understand: how to say *I forget.* It could be in my blood, but elfelejtettem: finished forgetting already.

She Doesn't Understand

A neighbor across the courtyard threw a jar of tomatoes at guests leaving our apartment because locals are day drinkers on their national holidays they don't like to stay up late in the morning Colin asked me to interpret the last time I was delighted by helping a man doors opened housewives scolded in French as well as if my Nem ertem meant *I don't see the problem* rather than *I don't know the words you are using.*

Ice Cubes in the Shape of Stars

1.
Although you produce
constant ruination,

you also produce

a squinting Orion,
an unlikely result.

When you slice
the eyeball, the

viewer matures.

2.
See how film
threatens style?

My target replaces
your panache.

It's an act that

fills the afternoon:
hot, quick, melting—

No, more sexual, more
details like fetishist,
like cellophane.

Explicit as brilliant
will allow.

Montage Our Way Through Winter

I'll use my *get out of jail free* card
and my good credit. A stranger
called me a whore in the subway
I saw a rat I got lonely I bought shoes
and ate ice cream I drank all the coffee
so I made more and I slept it all off.

You didn't call today. But if we
montage our way through winter,
I can wear my Little House on
the Prairie boots while we pretend
we do real work like chopping wood
or boiling pails of water, and I'll lift
my skirt to step over a puddle just
for the ceremony. There will be
moody string music and my hair
will go a little gray.

Would you like to be a power couple?
I'll pick you up at the airport in your
favorite kind of car. We'll circle things
to buy in a big catalog. You can get that
dog you want and name him Tobias.
Come spring, we could arrive in a new town
and between your neckties and my rhetoric,
we'd run a successful mayoral campaign.
You think I'm joking. Don't laugh at me.

The Same Sound Every Night

Am I elegant and unemployed? Yes,
and this season is meant for my looking
out from rooftops, for spreading out on
a picnic blanket myself. I cut through
the park carrying a bag of tangerines,
a carton of blueberries that would be
expensive back home. I can walk around
here all day eating fruit, watching various
creatures approach their warren, their
burrow at homecoming, up the escalator
to buses with broken headlights. The long
commute home is compelled by an
instinct I have not yet cultivated.

Certainty was supposed to come
on the evening of Manhattanhenge.
My friend said *you should be able
 to see the sun from where you are.*
An epiphany happens when the sunset
lines up with the street grid, but
I couldn't find the horizon, though
I walked fast until the warehouses
turned gray at the north tip of Greenpoint.
Time is titanic; when it is night already,
the neighborhood kids go on kiwi-eating
as I walk home. Music plays, but
the lights are out—a circuit is blown
and I still hear the same sound every night.
I aspire to heal bruises with oranges
alchemically, alone as if I am
the only unpossessable and blue one.

Blacker Birds

1.
Someone is always
bitching about

how black feathers are
actually purple, that language

belongs, that texture
exaggerates the signs,

how we know
what to dig and what
to cut up & when to stretch

my tone until you
feel the ribs.

2.
I pulled an idea
taut, snipped so

that black bell was
my black possession.

SALVAGE

The Imagined Affairs

I learned a new language to go to a new place over the yellow line of the subway my shoes soaked through on the way to the National Gallery I learned a new word— ruined—which echoed and I had to throw them out when we met for goulash my former teacher expected me to date him I used to ride my bike up Andrassy Street some new places echo my former teacher expected me to agree it was extremely hard to part with my American shoes.

Your mother tongue is impossible and without fluency what's lost in translation is at the root. Your sister complied when I said *promise you'll love me forever* she knew it wasn't binding. The principle of conservation of energy doesn't apply to dying languages. Nuanced terminology disappears. The fantasy spoils itself.

Diagnostic

He said *you eat like an American* and it's true that when we were homesick Suzanna and I ate Burger King in front of the television watching Red Bull commercials in Hebrew. She thought it was funny how *happy* was boldog, sounds like *bulldog*, while her nickname meant *virgin*. We took our recycling to the bins at the park and a man helped us drink the last sip in all the beer bottles we'd put our Gauloises out in the night before.

To Your Health

Of course words connected to alcohol are dizzying. You had a drinking glass cracked nearly all the way around, and I warned you would cut your mouth. Egészségedre and eye contact are mandated for a toast: egészség for *health*, ed for *your*, re for *to:* a waterfall of suffixes. You filled it with wine and drank it down to prove you could. Then I took the glass and snapped it in half for you, *brother*, testvér, which is a compound word: *fleshblood.*

Borderlands

Before the Treaty of Trianon was signed, I would have been having sex in Hungary rather than Romania. In the Kalotaszeg region where everyone makes pálinka in the backyard, where a particular kind of embroidery is practiced, we snuck out of the bar to fuck while *G.I. Jane* played in the next room, dubbed. Transylvania is bigger than you think—Dracula's castle was another sixteen hours away and I skipped sunrise over the Danube to act like a girlfriend. A lackluster performance.

Gift Economy

At Christmas my teacher gave me a bundle of twigs wrapped in a red bow said in Hungary it's used *to remind children of punishment* like a lump of coal in a stocking batted my hands a few times to demonstrate I saved the twigs in a shoebox for six years and when Kevin saw me open the box he said *Is that memory lane? No one keeps memory lane in a shoebox in the trunk of their car* I did and I included the jewelry I shoplifted from Wal-Mart although I'd never worn it.

Negotiation Phase

My Christian friend with a husband in Iraq hijacked a college boy's Chrysler to get me a steak burrito I passed out donating blood gave my ponytail to a group that makes wigs for children with cancer I don't need all those pints of blood those ponytails the charity of it made my teacher confess he cut up his face falling down drunk on his own street and his sister had an abortion though they're Catholic he thought I must love him back because I was a Democrat he asked on two continents.

The Future of Bad Times

You are the miracle from nowhere, Miss 19th Century. We've known since you were just former Little Miss Napoleonic. Such mismatched unblemished pittances you bore, too much for our Mr. Urban Outrage today. He's been persuaded to usher you in as yet another source of national pride. Bargain basement prices must be acknowledged and given their due, which is to say we're in utter denial of The Future of Bad Times. Do not bend to indulge your immanent tendency toward pessimistic overdose as this would be a mistake. Do not cement your reputation as misstepping sales agent. Keep clean. Mr. Current Administration wishes to inform you that when the century turns next, you'll need to rescind your crown and status, both the chopping block and ribbons for braiding. Your new job title will be something that means Old Miracle—not old, but Revered. Old Miracle Cheerleader: we're nearly certain that'll be you.

Excuse Me if I Break my Own Heart

My body wants to build another body that was ever afraid of a chain letter / that gets excited about the weather. My body wants to play but doesn't want to choke. The last good fuck my body is still waiting for it with a mouth open to express hunger sign says *our lost | your gain* my body, too, is awake / unemployed, interested in petty theft. My body watches too much wish-fulfillment reality television. Grabbing onto a manufactured body guarantees vanilla passage my body wants its identity stolen / its jewelry pawned. It stares into the mirrorback and nothing happens outside it is hailing / snowing and no adversity is to blame for this lack.

A *process* occurs when you give up your language and start calling things by new names but there's not a term for how new phrases infiltrate your reflex it starts with the gutturals and when you try to give it up try to back out the primal language dialects but you will understand shouts of surprise from the last place to wipe clean.

The Blues Are Merely More Complaint

I used to drive spokes
you'd torque
until

I meet a woman
she's a notary public

I hope she won't
notice
my dead batteries,

stacks of dishes,
          dirty underwear,

disgust at myself
so thick

I step over it

I hope
I never have to repair
          another machine

when I meet a woman
I won't have to try so hard

my documents will have
the most important seal

goodbye small claims court
my woman and I
          are making it official

The Galleria, Uptown Houston

This poem is better than yours
Providence, White-Hot Indignance: two new illusions

"I just want to go to the mall   and have a good time"
You want to watch all the ugly people   like I like

a threat to the grandfather clause   weaknesses are manifold
the bar and grill is present   let's graze

Becca's mother orders lemon drop martinis
          drinking at noon feels   tax-deductible

I feel the window frame   I need to touch glass
but it's open-air statistics: annual   consumption, origins

leisure is not enough   they anticipated us; pages of sod
trucked in to fill the median,   trees wrapped like lollipops

A red glow retreats   headlight approaches by margins
the size of a Polaroid aperture   the gulf remains unbridged

Pretend you are a Prairie locomotive   blow your whistle
plow the shoppers   stare back unironically

quit singing along with the radio   hard to disengage
from merciless gazing   I'm losing my commerce buzz

Working the System

It means tackling
the old arranged network
from the inside,
resisting mere iteration

You are:
        trills
        a cinched & neat parade salute
        patriotic pleasant ruffles
        perked and most open.

On occasion, battle will be necessary.
Take it as another fluid affair, a natural
extension. Make it look easy.

Meanwhile, people you used to know
will overcrush, pursuing a miracle.
Needing your heart.

Understand, delicate?
Be careful not to doubt your own ascendance.

It means the din of words to be ignored.
Become expatriate. Calculate exact,
then ignore examination. Exit,
rather, exculpate yourself.

Diamond Tattoo

I was having a Little Red Hen moment, who I thought
was called Henny Penny, but when I googled Henny Penny
I got Chicken Little. It was not a sky-is-falling moment,
but an I-will-eat-the-bread-myself one. Who will help me
harvest the wheat? Volunteerism is its own punishment.
I don't know why anyone would say no to you, old lover
offers. Who will help me bake the bread?

       I said Placido Polanco's name in my sleep,
       but I still can't find a date to a baseball game.

That old guy at the bar was right; my name means
I'm a diamond in the rough, my own best friend.
Like the eighth grade cover band doing "Polly Want a Cracker"
on the first anniversary of Kurt Cobain's death, how the guitarist
repeated "tragically," a crystal goblet of Fancy Feast is forever.

       Try writing a sentence that isn't a definition.

So impatient, any time I played *NBA Jam* I'd smash the
backboard as often as I could, desirous for cartoon glass.

Our Songs

are about hard-earned blank stares
or the tulip bulbs I plant while you mow

You clip stems too close to dirt,
except you want to touch dirt

We ruin our yard in slow lines
past the window for planting

We dig against the garage plasterboard
A mouse punctures leftover seeds

Later, our songs will steal the dim light
from your teeth during the real night,

which bothers us both tremendously
though I'll try to stay on the down low

First I knew poison, then passive aggression
A marathon is proof of your masochism

CONTINUUM

He Was Stapled, He Was Sewn

My mother thinks of her father as damaged because his heartbeat is irregular so I know what she'll think of my diabetic boyfriend. Sickness is a mistake to her. She's angry to read any diagnosis, but I can't muster it up you can't argue genetics. Still, hearing someone cough hard I think *give me a break already*. Illness as a matter of will, dying as weakness of character, (sub)urban legend.

He is afraid of bridges and needles but logged ten days in the hospital waiting over Labor Day then his birthday because doctors don't work weekends hospitals can't afford on the ninth day mother reports that my grandmother snapped at the nurses *That's not how you get what you want* I told her she protested it was unfair someone needs to announce *Don't look down* (at the needle) I said Happy Birthday in Hungarian, magyarul, the language I used to study. But in the hospital he spoke only English.

My Magenta Error-Proof Test

The job is to whisper into teenagers' ears about time, the next twenty minutes—the part of the future I know about. Because of one Depo Provera shot, I might not get my period for a year so I sit neutered but not safe reading about the Federal Reserve I may sit behind this desk forever if I have to explain why I went on the needle then you're right to disappear. I need to be your own only disaster I am afraid of the economy but keep going public like an animal that doesn't learn: a teacup chihuahua or a cat with no tail. I'm a mouse that thinks it's a china shop in a bull market.

Save These Instructions

Three men were not well and one died but not the one I thought would doesn't matter now another cascade suddenness literally ashes not only is it possible it's a fact if one dies then my entire family will which is obvious the next time I get a Google Alert with my full name it better not be another obituary if so I will need someone to slowly feed me a handful of candy I will be childlike and difficult.

Extreme situational juxtaposition or incongruity followed by specific details then a short anecdote that brings in another voice or character. Rhetorical question or general statement. Return to specificity from beginning, but with modulation. Surprising use of simile or metaphor, disregard secondary characters in favor of meaningful interiority: idea, image, epiphanic zinger.

Your Blood Like an Animal

Sleep alone every night for three months then share room with sister panic just like summer she rolls over unconscious I call *are you ok?* she doesn't know why I spoke no memory of it but certainly was your seizure ghost your jaw clamp and tongue blood pouring from mouth ghost that still wakes me up gives me night sweats suppressed images of coma watch: conditions always favorable for sudden sleepdeath. Now you do what you like with your teeth.

Price Point

The richest girl in La Mesilla wrote a book about the pond where the crack addicts and pederasts loiter across the street from the truck stop where I ate chicken fried steak every night I was drunk one summer but you don't have to be born here to appropriate the language and water has caught fire in bigger cities. During the presidential campaign we played stickball across the arroyo from a Republican rally noisy with recordings of white men playing guitars.

Dia de los Muertos flavored coffee and mugs with cartoon Billy the Kids retired couples on road trips picking hollyhocks from our yard so what could we do but drink and eat and smash wine glasses with a golf club? Destruction either internal or external, but something had to crumble: the jail the Kid was held in, the brothel-turned-restaurant, our house. The news out of Las Cruces lately is all catfight and lighter fluid but you can't write about the barrio if you lived on the compound. No points awarded.

The Sadder It Becomes

The father cut the cord at each child's birth and I babysat mean and bored worried the kids with reminders about vitamins and homework feeding the dog late that night he pawed and pawed at his bed worked to get it right the mother warned me never to change my name *changing it back is such a hassle* she moved to Texas to buy a car and date a doctor who would make her want to be sober.

Picked up his youngest daughter from a party when he was too drunk at ours to do it himself pretended to her it was normal she and I both knew better and that was fine. He dated students supposedly appropriate because of this or that ethical loophole never once tried to fuck the babysitter how I got to be the favorite stayed over with the kids one night the week I gave myself two black eyes.

Túró Rudi

In the bean-shaped hotel pool with palm tree on bottom you shirtless glossy turned into a whole fervent meal analogy for the quark cheese covered in chocolate only available in Hungary—must be refrigerated—Americans move there, marry citizens for access to one brand of candy wanted I left a note for the bookstore clerk who recognized me later when an old woman was kissing me on the mouth at the bar, you told me.

Unsatisfactory Progress

We move to Hattiesburg I go to beauty school we get rural I get licensed. My back hurts from bending over to wax women and departmental drama implodes as soon as he signs a contract our apartment has radical Southern bugs the unknowable *you can be scared or you can be ready* a false dilemma: beauty school or nothing he wants someone to take his name but doesn't want to get married. I know a list of contradictions doesn't add up to a poem of any substance but my temptation is great.

Burgeoning academic he throws in the term *new historicism* while we argue and snickers at himself abortion is new historicism. He'll believe in anything his least reliable mentor tells him, obviously didn't date me for the partner benefits. I choose getting neighborhoody while he gets all interstate highway I choose hair dye and lipstick but he'd rather sweat on someone new.

Lease Breaking

I got the deposit back after I filled the holes
        you put in the walls. No locks on the basement

windows, no lights beyond the kitchen. Swept
        the dead cicadas off the porch for our party

so no one had to drag their red eyes across
        the carpet. There must be bird people like

cat and dog people. The next street over,
        neighbors tire of hearing how *tweet tweet*

carries when you set traps for me. How else
        could there be birds and cages both?

You saw a deer run through the yard.
        We kept the sledgehammer by the back door,

the mud room. You can't catch a mouse
        that way, but you could scare a bird back

into its cage, you could hold that hammer
        under its beak and make it say *please.*

Urban Blight

At ten o'clock each night, the metal
        screeches down

Days marked off in scratched or rubber frictions
made of effort:

        use the peephole
        find he's squatter than he sounds
        whistle like you're hunting ducks
        throw your voice

Words on paper blur and
my vision dissolves as summer passes

A gnat in my periphery becomes
            a hammer swinging down

        Foreign cities make me this phobic
I know I won't come back

The only place open on this block
sells toilet paper, but not Coca-Cola

Building noise is how to speak to strangers
Pull the door shut quickly:

        the bag
        your wrist
        the door
        the neighbor
        his bicycle
        the last step

Welcome to Poetry City

I dream I'm big & pregnant and my water breaks
in the English department office, in the thesis library,

and the nice professor & the mean one call a truce just to coach
me into labor. I've never been pregnant so I don't know

if the dream is realistic, but its lack of subtlety disgusts me.
The conflict traveled with me like a burr and so I notice

a bar in my new neighborhood shares its name with the mean one.
I imagine sending her a t-shirt embossed with her own name. She

could wear it and lament *the size is too small / too big / just right.*
What unfinished business would you resolve? I'd forgive

her for her unhappiness, but not the lousy title suggestions.
When you bet against despair, you're only putting your money on

a different version; knowing as much I was never hysterical,
not in the dream or since. But if you think of reconciliation,

you presume the other party is amenable. She is not. Her anger
is her sticking point; it guarantees you'll never get another Christmas

card. She knows that gambling is a hobby practiced in solitude,
and works to maintain it. Scorn is an adhesive. It binds her to herself.

You Will Collect Leaky Rowboats

before you forget
why you walked into this room

peel the stamps off those chain letters
        and glue them to your manuscript

pawn what you find in the lost & found
        to buy more postage

you know the bakery throws out bagels
the same time every night   gather

reuse envelopes for distributing your manifesto
        better
        return solicitations to sender pre-paid

terrorize   demonstrate
                that commitment to nature
                means eating weeds in the park

once you figure out how to get a hose
down in the gas tank

that's when you'll think

                "deny, deny"

rent free   grey water—

        when you use a bathtub
you pee in the bathtub

Flesh: A Clarification

You cross your legs like Truman Capote
makes me think how   boys are abducted in rural China,

their meat so valuable it's trafficked
                    like steaks   or cocaine.

When they open their mouths,   money spills out.

Will it sputter?   Spray like I do
when I wake up swallowing blood?

Panic is what my veins feel, my skin feels.

Your knees stacked on top of each other,

you are a compressed scarecrow   explaining
how one word means both
                    dry hump   & *gravestone rubbing.*

I saw the Max Ernst exhibit
        I have to tell you:
                frottage is spelled this way,

        more French than you thought.

Suggestions for Longevity

You shouldn't try to feed the animals at the zoo.

This is how people keep getting mauled—ignoring the worry impulse, imagining animals are children.

I understand; sometimes I'm at the zoo, and I am the zoo.

An animal doesn't achieve domestication through meticulous planning, so *tame* applies to nothing.

Blame nature. No one will notice that it doesn't make any sense.

Winter creeper, kudzu ivy: with blooms, poisons are concomitant. Invasive species are a scourge.

Take things that look pretty and install them in new light.

But once everyone has tulips in their yard, then no one wants tulips anymore. Diminishing returns is basic economics.

Excise any wasteful habits. No more open tabs at the bar. No more cash advances. Cultivate a taste for comparison shopping.

The history of your movements and decisions will be dense.

What makes you less apt to eat wildflowers, weeds, garbage? The prevalence of citrus; your civilized interest in soups.

I'm set on ruining you now. Spell the president's name right.

Ignore research that proves deterioration is random. If you sneak around for drinks, you'll sneak for sex, too. You should control the particle that makes you mean.

You'll want to think the end isn't your fault. Get organized. Go for a hike. Start a non-profit.

I don't do that kind of thing, but I'm not the one who wants to live forever.

Krystal Languell was a semi-finalist for the 2010 University of Akron Press Poetry Prize and a finalist for the 2011 National Poetry Series. Her work has appeared in Denver Quarterly, Fairy Tale Review, and DIAGRAM among other journals, and was anthologized in the 2010 edition of Best of the Web. Founder the feminist literary magazine Bone Bouquet, she serves as a collaborative board member for Belladonna* Series as well as editor-in-chief at Noemi Press. She teaches composition at York College in Queens and the Borough of Manhattan Community College. She lives in Brooklyn, where she also co-curates the HOT TEXTS Reading Series.

Made in the USA
Monee, IL
07 July 2026